WHY DO ANIMALS GO There?

Jonathan Rosen

Rourke
Educational Media

rourkeeducationalmedia.com

Scan for Related Titles
and Teacher Resources

Teaching Focus:

Concepts of Print: Have students find capital letters and punctuation in a sentence. Ask students to explain the purpose for using them in a sentence.

Before Reading:

Building Academic Vocabulary and Background Knowledge

Before reading a book, it is important to set the stage for your child or student by using pre-reading strategies. This will help them develop their vocabulary, increase their reading comprehension, and make connections across the curriculum.

1. Read the title and look at the cover. *Let's make predictions about what this book will be about.*
2. Take a picture walk by talking about the pictures/photographs in the book. Implant the vocabulary as you take the picture walk. Be sure to talk about the text features such as headings, Table of Contents, glossary, bolded words, captions, charts/diagrams, and Index.
3. Have students read the first page of text with you then have students read the remaining text.
4. Strategy Talk – use to assist students while reading.
   - Get your mouth ready
   - Look at the picture
   - Think…does it make sense
   - Think…does it look right
   - Think…does it sound right
   - Chunk it – by looking for a part you know
5. Read it again.
6. After reading the book complete the activities below.

Content Area Vocabulary
Use glossary words in a sentence.

herbivores
matriarch
migration
resources
spawn
swarm

After Reading:

Comprehension and Extension Activity

After reading the book, work on the following questions with your child or students in order to check their level of reading comprehension and content mastery.

1. *What happens to salmon after they swim upstream to spawn?* (Summarize)
2. *How far do gray whales swim every year?* (Asking questions)
3. *Why does the matriarch lead an elephant herd?* (Inferring)
4. *Name three mammals that migrate.* (Summarize)

Extension Activity

Do you know people who have moved to a new home or new city? Think of everyone you know who's moved, and their reasons for moving. Then, think of all the reasons people might need to move. How are their reasons the same or different from animals who move, or migrate?

Table of Contents

Birds of a Feather

When you hear the word **migration**, what animals do you think of? Birds often come to mind!

As the weather turns cold, **resources** disappear. For birds, that means less food to eat.

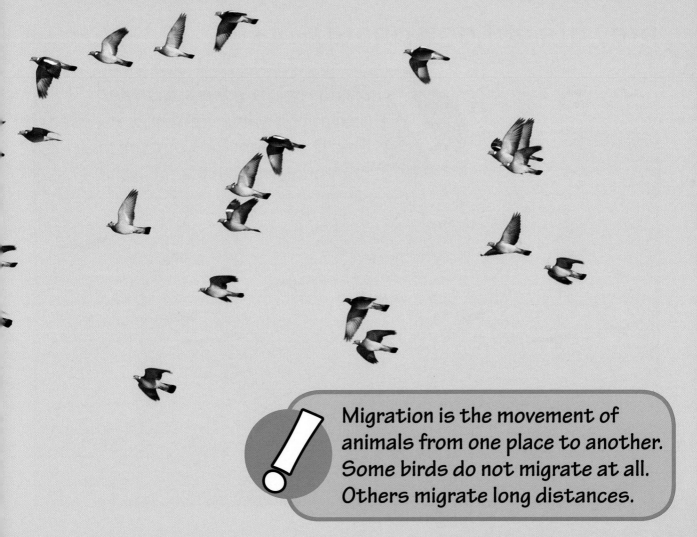

Migration is the movement of animals from one place to another. Some birds do not migrate at all. Others migrate long distances.

Some Northern Hemisphere birds will fly south for the winter to look for food. It's warmer there. This means more tasty prey are out and about!

Birds fly in a V formation and travel the same routes every year. This lets them look out for and communicate with each other.

Animals also migrate for breeding. Every March in Antarctica, Emperor penguins travel 60 to 100 miles (95.6 to 160 kilometers) inland. Once there, females lay eggs and males sit on them.

Mammal Migration

Birds aren't the only animals that migrate. Many mammals do too. Deer leave snow-covered areas in the winter to look for places with lots of grass.

 Nobody knows for sure how animals know where to go when they migrate. Some scientists think they follow the position of the stars. Others think animals are born with their migration habits and routes established.

African zebras are constantly on the move. They travel from the Serengeti into Kenya and back again, in a giant clockwise circle, following the seasons of rain.

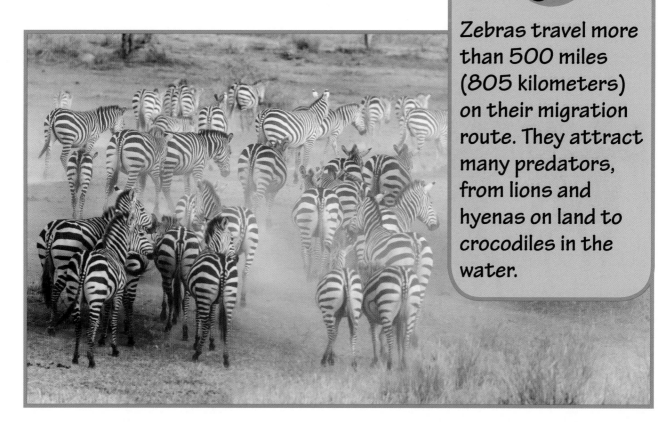

Zebras travel more than 500 miles (805 kilometers) on their migration route. They attract many predators, from lions and hyenas on land to crocodiles in the water.

Zebras travel with millions of other **herbivores**, such as wildebeests.

Elephant migrations are led by the **matriarch** of the herd. Another older female takes a position at the back of the line. They watch for predators and make sure the younger elephants are fed.

Traveling Insects

Every fall, millions of Monarch butterflies leave their cold northern climate behind. They travel more than 2,000 miles (3,219 kilometers) to the warmth of southern California or Mexico.

The Monarch is the only butterfly known to make a two-way migration, just like birds do.

Millions of locusts **swarm** together. They can travel up to 100 miles (161 kilometers) a day, destroying crops along the way.

Migrating dragonflies follow the same path as birds, along the Atlantic seaboard.

Some ladybugs migrate in the cold weather. In Oregon, they will head for the mountains.

Just Add Water

Gray whales swim more than 5,000 miles (8,047 kilometers) every year. They travel from cold waters by the Bering Sea to warm waters by Baja, California, to give birth to their calves.

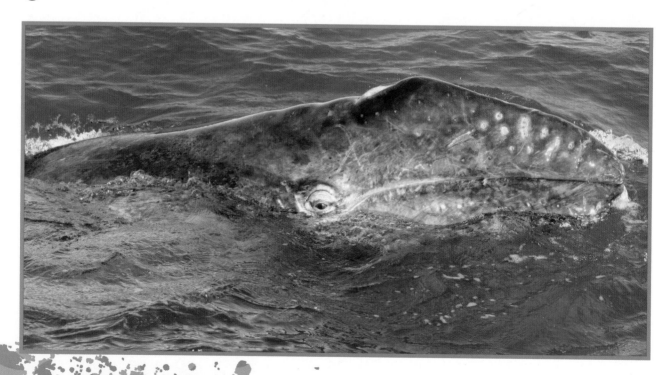

Every fall, salmon swim upstream
from the ocean saltwater to freshwater
riverbeds to **spawn**, or release their eggs.

European eels do the opposite of salmon. They swim from freshwater rivers to saltwater seas to spawn.

Sea turtles return to the same beach where they hatched to lay their own eggs.

Scientists haven't figured out how sea turtles know the way back to their birthplace. It's a mystery!

Every October, on Christmas Island, red crabs travel from the forest to the coast to release their eggs. The eggs hatch when they come in contact with sea water.

The residents of Christmas Island close the roads to let the red crabs safely make their journey.

During rainy seasons, frogs return to mate in the swamps where they were born. The males go first and call to the females by croaking.

Photo Glossary

herbivores (HUR-buh-vors): Animals that eat only plants.

matriarch (may-TREE-ark): A mother who is the head of the family.

migration (mye-GRAY-shuhn): The movement of people or animals from one region or habitat to another.

resources (REE-sors-ez): Something that is of value or use, such as food and shelter.

spawn (spawn): To produce a large number of eggs.

swarm (sworm): A group of insects that gather or move in large numbers.

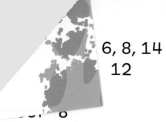

Websites to Visit

animals.mom.me

www.nationalgeographic.com

www.earthrangers.com

Meet The Author!
www.meetREMauthors.com

About the Author

Jonathan Rosen is a writer living in Coral Springs, Florida, with his family. He is a contributing writer to FromtheMixedUpFiles.com. He coaches his children in sports and helps them with their homework. Well, except for math, because that's really hard. He has lived all over the world, and hopes to eventually find a place that will let him stay.

Library of Congress PCN Data

Why Do Animals Go There?/ Jonathan Rosen
(Why Do Animals...)
ISBN 978-1-68191-723-8 (hard cover)
ISBN 978-1-68191-824-2 (soft cover)
ISBN 978-1-68191-918-8 (e-Book)
Library of Congress Control Number: 2016932647

Rourke Educational Media
Printed in the United States of America, North Mankato, Minnesota

© 2017 Rourke Educational Media

www.rourkeeducationalmedia.com

Edited by: Keli Sipperley
Cover design, interior design and art direction: Nicola Stratford

PHOTO CREDITS: Cover © Oleg Znamenskiy; page 4-5 © Scandphoto; page 6-7 © Jearu, page 7 © Bernard Breton | Dreamstime.com; page 8 © Lorraine Logan, page 9 © Mark52; page 10 © Efimova Anna, page 11 © 2630ben; page 12 © JHVEPhoto, page 13 © Vladimir Wrangel; page 14 © Tania Adamus, page 15 © ItsAngela; page 16 © James Michael Dorsey; page 17 © Sekar B; page 18 © Mikelane45 | Dreamstime.com, page 19 © David Evison; page 20 © DIAC images, page 21 © fastfun23 All photos from Shutterstock.com except pages 7 and 18 Dreamstime.com and page 20

Also Available as:

ROURKE'S e-Books